"Servile Ministers": *Othello, King Lear*
and the Sacralization of Service

Frontispiece of George Gascoigne's Hemetes the Heremyte,
with the author presenting his book to the Queen, c. 1576.

"Servile Ministers":

Othello, King Lear and the

Sacralization of Service

THE 2003 GARNETT SEDGEWICK

MEMORIAL LECTURE

Michael Neill

RONSDALE PRESS

VANCOUVER

Ronsdale Press
3350 West 21st Avenue
Vancouver, B.C., Canada
V6S 1G7

Set in Minion: 11 on 15
Typesetting: Julie Cochrane
Printing: The Printing House Ltd., Vancouver, B.C., Canada
Cover Design: Julie Cochrane
Front Cover Art: Ambassadorial Service — the Moorish Ambassador to Queen
    Elizabeth, English School, early seventeenth century.
Back Cover Art: Engraving by Georg Hoefnagel of Queen Elizabeth in an open
    coach proceeding to Nonsuch Palace, c. 1582.

Ronsdale Press wishes to thank the Canada Council for the Arts, the Government
of Canada through the Book Publishing Industry Development Program (BPIDP),
and the Province of British Columbia through the British Columbia Arts Council
for their support of its publishing program.

NATIONAL LIBRARY OF CANADA CATALOGUING IN PUBLICATION

Neill, Michael
    "Servile ministers": *Othello, King Lear* and the sacralization
of service / Michael Neill.

(Garnett Sedgewick memorial lecture 2003)
Includes bibliographical references.
ISBN 1-55380-015-X

    1. Shakespeare, William, 1564–1616. Othello. 2. Shakespeare, William, 1564–1616.
King Lear. 3. Master and servant in literature.
I. Title. II. Series.
PR3069.S43N45 2004   822.3'3   C2003-906869-2

FOR
KUBÉ

INTRODUCTION

The first of the Sedgewick Lectures was given in 1955, six years after Dr. Sedgewick's death. Since then, distinguished speakers such as Philip Akrigg, Hugh MacLennan, Northrop Frye, Robert Bringhurst, Sandra Djwa, and William H. New have explored various topics from "Native American Oral Literatures and the Unity of the Humanities" to "Grandchild of Empire: About Irony, Mainly in the Commonwealth." Dr. Michael Neill from Auckland, New Zealand, continues this fine series with his lecture on "'Servile Ministers': *Othello, King Lear* and the Sacralization of Service."

The Sedgewick lectures are named in honour of Garnett G. Sedgewick, the first Head of the Department of English at the University of British Columbia, whose influence is still felt in the Department today. Dr. Sedgewick was hired by the University of British Columbia in 1918, and two years later became Head of the English Department, a post which he retained to 1948. He laid the foundations for the Department in the 1920's, nurtured it through the Depression years in the 1930's, and presided over its rapid expansion after World War II. Despite his administrative activities he found time for scholarship as well. His main area of scholarly interest was Shakespeare, and his reputation was such that he was invited to give the Alexander Lectures at the University of Toronto in 1934. These lectures have subsequently been published under the title *Of Irony: Especially in Drama*. By all accounts, Dr. Sedgewick was an outstanding teacher, a fabulous mentor to his students, and a man who deeply cared about the world around him, the latter being most evident in the semi-weekly column he wrote for the *Vancouver Sun* from September 1936 to October 1937, and which he ironically entitled "More Light than Heat."

With this year's lecturer, Dr. Michael Neill, we return to the interests central to Dr. Sedgewick. Dr. Neill teaches at the English Department of the University of Auckland; he is a Renaissance specialist and has published widely on sixteenth- and seventeenth-century drama. His books include *Issues of Death: Mortality and Identity in English Renaissance Tragedy* (1997) and *Putting History to the Question: Power, Politics, and Society in English Renaissance Drama* (2000). Dr. Neill has also published a scholarly edition of *Anthony and Cleopatra* (1994), not to mention numerous learned articles. Recently he has returned to his roots as editor and is — among other things — currently working on the Oxford edition of *Othello*.

This most concentrated mulling over every word of *Othello* gives rise in part to this year's lecture, which asks the question as to the meaning of the terms "servant" and "slave" in the early modern period. Dr. Neil examines the Bible and booklets on household government, applies his findings to the Shakespearean works, and arrives at astonishing conclusions. "I'll never be able to look at the words 'slave' and 'servant' the way I used to," said one member of the audience after the lecture. Readers, I have no doubt, will find this lecture similarly full of insights.

— Gernot R. Wieland
Professor and Head

"SERVILE MINISTERS":
OTHELLO, KING LEAR AND THE
SACRALIZATION OF SERVICE

In the course of the great speech of self-justification with which he defends himself to the Venetian Senate, Othello recalls how he was "taken by the insolent foe, / And sold to slavery" (1.3.6–7).[1] But at the end of the play, in an irony that usually passes unnoticed, it is the Moor's triumphant antagonist, Iago, who is branded — not once, but four times — as a "slave" (5.2.241, 275, 289, 338). Iago's brand is not literal, of course; for "slave" had become one of the most common (as well as potent) terms of abuse in the extensive repertory of status-based insult that adorned the early modern lexicon. In *King Lear* it is the word which the King uses to denounce another treacherous subordinate — the compliant Officer who performs his murderous "man's work" on Cordelia: "I killed the *slave* that was a-hanging thee" (5.3.274); it is also the word with which Lear and Kent repeatedly debase Goneril's overweening steward, the "super-serviceable" Oswald (1.4.55, 86; 2.2.17–18, 41–42, 73; 2.4.187, 218); it is the word that concentrates Cornwall's sense of outrage, when his own servant stands up against the blinding of Gloucester: "Throw this slave upon the dunghill" (3.7.95); it is the word that expresses Oswald's disgust when he is overcome by the disguised Edgar: "Slave, thou hast slain me" (4.6.247); and it is the word with which the King describes his own degraded condition on the heath, when exposed to the power of elements that in turn appear to function as

---

[1] Unless otherwise indicated, all references to *Othello* are to the Penguin edition, ed. Kenneth Muir (Penguin: Harmondsworth, 1968), whilst all references to *King Lear* are to the Arden edition, ed. Kenneth Muir (Methuen: London, 1964); emphases, however, are my own.

"servile ministers" of his daughters' will: "You owe me no subscription: then let fall / Your horrible pleasure; here I stand, your slave" (3.2.19–21). The very frequency of the term means that modern readers are likely to brush over it as a vague hyperbole — especially as it seems unanchored to a recognisable social context either inside or outside the plays. After all, the institution of slavery had no significant place in the English social order; nor (despite the efforts of John Hawkins in the 1560s) had the Atlantic slave-trade yet become a major source of English mercantile wealth.[2] Pre-Roman Britain may have been a slave-owning society, but slavery seems, if anything, even more remote from Lear's Britain than from Othello's Venice. Othello himself may have been "sold to slavery," but that can easily seem part of his exotic "travel's history," along with "Anthropophagi and men whose heads / Do grow beneath their shoulders" (1.3.137).[3] His enslavement hardly seems to impinge on the self-confident character we are shown in the play, nor does it have much to do with the world he presently inhabits: perhaps these Venetians, like Shylock's persecutors, keep amongst them "many a purchased slave";[4] but, if so, we hear nothing of it.

Nevertheless, it is clear that both plays are profoundly concerned with an institution that bore an obvious relation to slavery — namely service. The two terms, one standing for voluntary and the other for involuntary subordination, define two modes of social being, and ultimately two kinds of society. In *Othello,* it is on the

---

[2] For some discussion of the significance of the term in early modern culture, see Camille Wells Slights, "Slaves and Subjects in *Othello,*" *Shakespeare Quarterly* 48 (1997), 377–90.

[3] In fact his slavery belongs not to the mercantile Atlantic triangle, but to the very different institution fostered by the struggle between Christianity and Islam in the Mediterranean — see Michael Neill, "'His Master's Ass': Slavery, Service, and Subordination in *Othello,*" forthcoming in Stanley Wells and Tom Clayton (eds.) *Shakespeare in the Mediterranean* (Newark: University of Delaware Press, 2003).

[4] *The Merchant of Venice,* 4.1.90, cited from the edition by W. Moelwyn Merchant (Harmondsworth: Penguin Book, 1967).

"service" that he has done the state that the Moor founds his claim to be "of Venice";[5] just as in *King Lear* it is his commitment to "service" that defines the dual identity of Kent/Caius. By the same token, it is their hypocritical betrayal of the bonds of service that marks the villains of the plays, reducing them to the moral status of slaves. Thus if we want to understand the insulting power that infuses the epithet "slave," it is to the discourse of service that we must turn.

As I have argued elsewhere, "service" in the early modern period was a remarkably inclusive concept, embracing in its most elastic definition virtually all forms of social relationship — since even the bonds between husbands and wives, parents and children involved the same principles of authority and obedience.[6] The ideological reach of the concept was guaranteed by the sacralized authority with which it was invested, in a world where the distinction between the sacred and the secular was by no means as clear as it appears to us. Then as now, of course, the term had a conspicuous application to sacred ritual — as in the description of formal worship as "divine service"; but that expression merely reflects the way in which the Christian subject's duty to God was imagined as the pattern of all servant-master relationships. By invoking God and Christ as the patterns not merely of paternal authority and filial

---

[5] Here Shakespeare seems to be remembering Contareni's remarks on service as a route to Venetian citizenship for foreigners: "Yea and some forrain men and strangers haue beene adopted into this number of citizens, eyther in regard of their great nobility, or that they had beene dutifull towardes the state, or els had done unto them some notable seruice", Gasparo Contareni, *The Commonwealth of Venice*, trans. Lewis Lewkenor (1599), 18.

[6] See Michael Neill, "Servant Obedience and Master Sins: Shakespeare and the Bonds of Service," in Neill, *Putting History to the Question: Power, Politics, and Society in English Renaissance Drama* (New York: Columbia University Press, 2000), 13–48. The close links between the obedience owed by wives and children is stressed in William Gouge's comprehensive manual of household government, *Of Domesticall Dvties Eight Treatises* (1622): "[although] a seruants place and dutie is of more abiect and inferiour kinde then the place and dutie of a childe or wife: the former word (. . . *obey*) was common to all" (168).

obedience, but of mastery and service, the official voice of early modern culture could present all domestic relationships as profoundly sacralized.[7] We can recognise this when Desdemona, invoking the sacrament of marriage, speaks of her "soul and fortunes" as "consecrate[d]" to her husband;[8] or when Lear humbles himself by kneeling to Cordelia in an inversion of the quotidian ritual of blessing through which fathers acted as the conduit of divine grace for their children. But it can be equally conspicuous in master-servant relationships: the shocking power of the improvised rite in which a kneeling Iago gives up "The execution of his wit, hands, heart, / To wronged Othello's service" (3.3.462–64) depends on its sacrilegious enactment of a sacred bond. In the patriarchal household, Peter Laslett has written, "every relationship could be seen as a love-relationship," and that love, as Iago's parody of nuptial vows suggests, was sacralized.[9]

In this context it is worth noticing that the idea of slavery in *Othello* is dressed with its own theologically weighted language: Othello speaks of his release from enslavement as "my *redemption* thence," whilst Iago is successively denounced by Montano, Othello, and Lodovico as a *"damned"* and *"cursed* slave." "Redemption," was of course, the usual term for purchasing the freedom of a slave or captive; but the powerful Christian connotations of the word are impossible to ignore when it is applied to the history of a Christianized Moor, just as the literal sense of "damned" inevitably attaches

---

[7] For a detailed account of ways in which the idea of divinely sanctioned service was propagated through Cranmer's Anglican liturgy, see David Evett, "Luther, Cranmer, Service, and Shakespeare," forthcoming in Daniel Doerksen and Christopher Hodgkins (eds.), *Centered on the Word: Literature, Scripture, and the Tudor-Stuart Middle Way* (Newark: University of Delaware Press, 2003).

[8] It is in this context that Desdemona can properly speak of the "rites" for which she loves her husband — rites that include the performance of all those duties that constituted wifely obedience.

[9] Peter Laslett, *The World We Have Lost — Further Explored*, 3rd edn. (London: Methuen, 1983), 5.

to a self-professed adherent of the "divinity of hell" like Iago (2.3.340), whom Othello half-believes a "devil" (5.2.284, 297). The neatness of this reversal is compromised, however, by the ambiguous reference of Othello's distracted cry, "cursed, cursed slave," which threatens to collapse the distinction between Iago and himself. If slavery is imagined as a reprobate state — the opposite of that "free condition" achieved by Othello's double redemption from slavery and paganism (1.2.26) — then it is into a new and worse slavery that the Moor is betrayed when having "curse[d] his better angel from his side ... [he] fall[s] to reprobance" (5.2.207–8). For, if the abject condition of the slave could stand for reprobation, the free performance of service, it turns out, could often resemble grace.

The Latin word *servus,* from which *servant* derives — and whose original connotations survive in such denigratory formations as *servile* — did not discriminate between slavery and free service; but Christian doctrine, with its insistence on equality before God and the freedom conferred by Christ had made the distinction all-important. "Art thou called being a seruant? Care not for it. . . . For he that is called in the Lord being a seruant, is the Lords freman: likewise also he that is called being fre, is Christs seruant" (1 Cor. 7.21–22); "we are not children of the seruant, but of the frewoman," he urges. "Stand fast therefore in the libertie wherwith Christ hath made us fre, and be not intangled againe with the yoke of bondage" (Gal. 4.31–5.1).[10] In place of the bondage to which humanity was consigned by the ruthless logic of sin and the Law, the new dispensation substituted the reciprocal "bandes in Christ" or "bondes of the Gospel" described in the Epistles (Phil. 1.13; Philem. 13).[11]

Conscious of the subversive potential of such doctrine in the

---

[10] All biblical quotations (except those cited via other sources) are from the 1560 Geneva Bible, the version best known to Shakespeare.

[11] For other scriptural formulations of the doctrine of free service, and its various elaborations by the Church fathers, medieval theologians, and Protestant reformers, see Evett, *op. cit.*

hands of radical sectaries, early theorists of service were quick to adapt the rhetoric of freedom to their own autocratic idea of household government. Thus William Gouge set out to rebut the Anabaptists, who, citing St Paul's "be not the seruants of men" (1 Cor. 7.23), had proclaimed that all "subiection of seruants to masters is against [Christian] prerogatiue," since "it is the prerogatiue of Christians to be all one" and "subiection is against the liberty that Christ hath purchased for vs . . . wherewith he hath made vs free."[12] Gouge, following the paradoxical insistence of the *Book of Common Prayer* that God's "service is perfect freedom,"[13] countered by citing an earlier verse in Corinthians and insisting that, since all service belongs to God, the true servant is always free:[14]

> Let there be cheerefulnesse in a seruants minde, and he is as free as his master: for such a seruant is *the Lords freeman* (1 Cor. 7.22) . . . and when he cannot be made free of his master, he doth after a manner make his seruice free.

Of course servants are "bound to obedience"; indeed "it is their main, and most popular function, to *obey their masters,*" whilst

> They who are contrary minded, who are rebellious, and disdain to be under the authority of another, and are ready to say of their Master, *We will not have this man to reigne over vs,* are fitter to live among Anabaptists, than orthodoxall Christians. For to what end is the lawfulness of authority acknowledged, if subjection be not yielded unto it?[15]

But such "subjection" is not to be confused with slavish bondage. In language that resonates with *King Lear's* emphasis on the "bonds" of service and filial duty, Gouge writes of "that neare bond which is betwixt master and seruants":

---

[12] Gouge, 593.

[13] See the Collect for Peace in the service of Morning Prayer. The sources of Cranmer's paradoxical formulation are discussed in Evett, *op. cit.*

[14] Gouge, 619.

[15] Gouge, 167, 618, 603–4.

Masters are as well bound to duties as seruants. Gods law requireth as much. . . . So doth also the law of nature which hath tied master and seruant together by mutuall and recipro-call bond, of doing good, as well as of receiuing good.[16]

The notion of service as a divinely sanctioned institution ap-peared to be underwritten in scripture not only by a number of parables in which God's relationship with humanity is analogised to that of a master with his servants, but even by the routine deploy-ment of secular honorifics such as "lord" and "master" in religious discourse. As such language suggested, the "mutuall and reciprocall bond" celebrated by Gouge, though founded in "a common equitie betwixt masters and seruants," did not involve any kind of "equal-itie."[17] It required instead a quasi-religious "dutie of reuerence" towards masters, since if Christ, by *"[taking] vpon him the forme of a seruant,"* offered the perfect ideal of willing service, he was also the pattern of all masters. Thus service, as St Paul had insisted, must be performed *"with feare and trembling in singlenesse of your heart, as vnto Christ"* (Ephesians 6.5); and although the *"[o]bedience which [servants] yeeld to their master must be such as may stand with their obedience to Christ,"* there should in theory be no conflict between sacred and profane duty. Since God was the supreme master from whom all authority derived, and the rebellious Lucifer the original of all disobedience, the faithful servant's fulfilment of his office was an expression of Christian duty, while any resistance to the master's command must be devilishly inspired; indeed Gouge went so far as to say that

> masters by vertue of their office and place beare Christs image, and stand in his stead, by communication of Christs authority to them they are called *Lords*, yea also *Gods* (for that which a Magistrate is in the Common-wealth a master is in the family). Hence it followeth that seruants in performing duty to their

---

[16] Gouge, 629, 171–72.

[17] Gouge, 173.

master performe duty to Christ, and in rebelling against their master, they rebell against Christ.[18]

Conservative, even reactionary, as Gouge's arguments may appear, they nevertheless chime with the idea of free service that more liberal thinkers, anxious to discard all relics of the "Norman yoke" had begun to develop as part of the myth of the "free-born Englishman." The role of slavery in this discourse was in essence rhetorical: by defining all that the servant was *not*, the abject bondage of the slave helped to sustain the idea of service as a system of voluntary engagement and profoundly naturalised "bonds" that constituted (however paradoxically) an expression of the free condition. Thus William Harrison, in his *Description of England* (1580), proclaimed that: "as for slaves and bondmen, we have none; nay, such is the privilege of our country by the especial grace of God and bounty of our princes, that if any come hither from other realms, so soon as they set foot on land they become so free of condition as their masters, whereby all note of servile bondage is removed from them."[19] In the words of the leveller John Lilburne (writing in 1652, but citing an Elizabethan case) England breathed "too pure an air for slaves to live in."[20] In some instances, of course, the distinction between service and slavery might seem an uncomfortably narrow one; but it was, all commentators agreed, essential. Thus Sir Thomas Smith's *De Republica Anglorum* (1583) acknowledged that "necessitie and want of bondmen hath made men to use free men and bondmen to all servile services: but yet more liberally and freely, and with more equalitie and moderation, than in time of gentilitie [i.e. pre-Christian times] slaves and bondmen were woont to be used" (98).[21]

---

[18] Gouge, 637, 124, 641.

[19] William Harrison, *Description of England* (1580), 118; cited in Robert J. Steinfeld, *The Invention of Free Labor: The Employment Relation in English and American Law and Culture, 1350–1870* (Chapel Hill: University of North Carolina Press, 1991), 97.

[20] Cited in Steinfeld, 97.

Shakespeare's own engagement with such paradoxes is conspicuously displayed in the schematic design that underlies the most visionary of his dramas, *The Tempest* — the play with which he seemingly planned to close his London career, and with which Heminge and Condell chose to open the First Folio. Crucial to the design of *The Tempest*, with its elaborate variations on the themes of service and freedom, is the contrast between the obedient servant Ariel and the refractory slave Caliban, in their struggle to win liberty from their overweening master, Prospero. Far from being inimical to freedom, however, service turns out to be the route to its attainment. At the centre of the play's action is a scene in which the captive Prince Ferdinand transforms his exhibition of "wooden slavery" to Prospero (3.1.62) into a proof of the humble service he vows to Miranda, offering it "with a heart as willing / As bondage e'er of freedom" (ll. 88–89).[22] Like Gouge's servant, whose acceptance of servitude "doth . . . make his service free," Ferdinand discovers freedom (as Ariel, and ultimately Prospero himself, will do) through submission: and this is what it will mean for Caliban (in the theologically loaded language with which he acknowledges Prospero as "my master") to "seek for grace" (5.2.262, 295).

Looking back to *Othello* and *King Lear,* we can see how the action of each of these plays turns on a similar contrast between free service and slavery. These two tragedies, though probably written no more than a year apart, are not often considered together: the narrow domestic focus of the former contrasts so sharply with the imaginative grandeur of the latter that they can seem to stand at opposite poles of Shakespeare's tragic range. Yet on one level, of

---

[21] Rather more equivocally, Edward Chamberlayne, in *Angliae Notitia* (1669) described apprentices as "a sort of servants that carry the marks of pure villains or Bond-slaves," but insisted that they "[differed] however in this, that Apprentices are slaves only for a time and by Covenant"; both cited in Steinfeld, *The Invention of Free Labor,* 98.

[22] See Neill, "Servant Obedience," 21–24, and Evett, *op.cit.* All citations from *The Tempest* are to the Arden edition, ed. Frank Kermode (London: Methuen, 1964).

course, *Lear* is a family drama in which the politics of the household are quite as important as those of the state; and in both plays it is the ideology of service that links the two domains. I am not, of course, the first to explore their common interest in what it means to be a servant. It was Jonas Barish and Marshall Waingrow who, forty years ago, first drew attention to the prominence of service in *Lear*: "Its presence [they wrote] is felt very strongly not only through the steady succession of incidents involving masters and servants, but even more pervasively through . . . reiteration [of the terminology of service]."[23] For all the persuasive detail of their analysis, however, Barish and Waingrow were troubled by an uneasy sense that "the theme of service is obvious . . . only in its presence, not in its meaning"; any attempt to formulate that meaning, they concluded, tended to stumble on "a number of intersecting paradoxes which effectively demolish a complacent reading."[24] These paradoxes involved both a deeply equivocal attitude towards the significance of rank, and a sense of the disturbing contradictions between socially sanctioned duties and moral obligation.

In a trenchantly argued essay, Richard Strier sought to account for the play's paradoxical attitudes towards rank and authority by linking them to Renaissance arguments about the limits of obedience — and in particular to the views advanced by sixteenth-century Protestant radicals like Ponet and Buchanan, who advocated resistance to tyranny as the path of Christian duty.[25] The servant who refused consent to his master's iniquity, Buchanan had argued — in an image that resonates powerfully with the medical language of Lear's restoration scene (4.7) — was "his master's true physician."[26]

---

[23] Jonas A. Barish and Marshall Waingrow, "'Service' in *King Lear*," *Shakespeare Quarterly* 9 (1958), 347–55 (348).

[24] Barish and Waingrow, *loc. cit.*

[25] Richard Strier, "Faithful Servants: Shakespeare's Praise of Disobedience," in Heather Dubrow and Richard Strier (eds.), *The Historical Renaissance: New Essays on Tudor and Stuart Literature and Culture* (Chicago: University of Chicago Press, 1988), 104–33.

[26] Strier, 110.

Courtly service: the visit of Queen Elizabeth to Blackfriars, 1600, from the painting by Marcus Gheerarts in the possession of the Earl of Ilchester at Melbury.

Strier traced Shakespeare's interest in "virtuous disobedience" back to *Othello,* discovering "the very threshold" of *King Lear* in Emilia's renunciation of her wifely duty to Iago: "'Tis proper I obey him, but not now" (5.2.193). From this point onwards, Strier argued, "Shakespeare consistently dramatized and espoused the most radical of [Ponet's and Buchanan's] ideas and placed them in a secular context."[27] Much of Strier's argument is entirely persuasive. However, it seems to me that, in his effort to identify Shakespeare with a secularised radicalism, he simplifies the dramatist's treatment of subordination and obedience, whilst largely discounting the social and theological context in which early modern arguments about the nature and limits of true service were conducted. In the process he disguises the extent to which the limits of obedience were a matter

---

[27] Strier, 111.

of concern not merely for radicals like Buchanan, but for social conservatives like William Gouge. Commenting upon St Paul's "be not the seruants of men" (1 Cor. 7.23), Gouge distinguished between true service and obsequious "excesse," arguing that the former would always place "Gods word and will" above the whims of an earthly master:

> *To be a seruant* in that place is not simply to be in subiection vnder another, and to doe seruice vnto him, but to be obsequious to a man, so addicted to please him, and so subiect to his will, as to doe whatsoeuer he will haue done: to regard nothing but his pleasure: to prefer it before Gods word and will. It is not therefore the thing it selfe, but an excesse therein which is forbidden.[28]

Shakespeare's propensity, in both *Othello* and *King Lear,* to push the paradoxes of obedience precisely to the point of "excesse" no doubt contributed to the gradual desacralization of service that Gouge was resisting. But far from adopting a consistent attitude to this process, the plays use it as an occasion for holding the ideology of service up to debate, and for exposing its painful contradictions: as always, Shakespeare seems more interested in questions than in doctrine, more concerned to stretch his audience upon the rack of doubt and uncertainty than to instruct them.

In the case of *Othello,* Emilia's gesture of disobedience cannot be detached from the play's larger treatment of duty and service, on which its theatrical power depends. In Shakespeare's Venice (as I have argued elsewhere)[29] faithful service is imagined as the very ground of social identity: Montano, the governor of Cyprus who yields his office to Othello as a master whom he is proud to have "served" (2.1.35–36), is defined by his role as the "trusty and most valiant servitor" of Venice (1.3.40); by the same token Cassio's self-image is completely inseparable from the "place" secured by "love

---

[28] Gouge, 593–94.

[29] See Neill, "Servant Obedience," and "'His Master's Ass'," cited above, nn. 5, 3.

and service" to his general (3.3.17–18). As "a member of [Othello's] love" (3.4.108), Cassio (like any good servant) imagines himself as an aspect of his master's countenance, a creature whose very being is contingent upon his continued capacity to perform "the *office* of [his] heart" (3.4.109).[30] No wonder that his plea for reinstatement is founded on an appeal to "service past" (3.4.117). In much the same way Desdemona sees her identity, formerly expressed in the filial obedience owed to her father, as contained in the wifely "duty . . . Due to the Moor, my lord" (1.3.182–87): what looks to Brabantio like an act of disobedience — something that the Duke sees as having "beguiled your daughter of herself" (1.3.66) — she herself justifies as a due transfer of allegiance, a reconstitution of self in which "My heart's *subdued* / Even to the very quality of my lord" (1.3. 247–48). It is this same sense of her identity as being properly subsumed in that of her husband that informs the paradoxical self-cancellation of Desdemona's last speech in the play, when she nominates herself as her own murderer: "Nobody — I myself . . . Commend me to my kind lord" (5.2.125–26). But it is Othello more than anyone who invests himself in the ideology of service and obedience: on his first appearance in the play, already stigmatized by Roderigo as "an extravagant and wheeling stranger / Of here and everywhere" (1.1.137–38), the Moor asserts his oxymoronic claim to be "of Venice" by appealing to "My *services* which I have done the signiory" (1.2.18); and at the point of death, when his Venetian self seems to have disintegrated into the unbeing of "he that *was* Othello" (5.2.281), he seeks to restore it with a defiant repetition of that claim — "I have done the state some *service,* and they know't" (5.2.335).

At the opposite extreme from those whose identity can be expressed only in the self-effacement of service is Iago, for whom it

---

[30] Compare John Dod and Robert Cleaver, *A Godly Forme of Household Government* (London, 1630), Sig. Aa3: "[G]ood and faithful servants, liking and affecting their masters . . . obey them . . . not as a water-spaniel, but as the hand is stirred to obey the mind." On the subsumption of the servant's identity in that of his master, see "Servant Obedience," 20–28.

is egotistically invested in the "power and corrigible authority" of his own will (1.3.322). Where Othello imagines his service to the state (in a secular version of the Christian paradox) as the very ground of his "free condition," Iago regards "service" as the euphemism in which authority cloaks the "obsequious bondage" of subordinate rank. His resentment fired by the inferior "place" to which his general has assigned him, he experiences the performance of any subordinate office as a form of humiliating enslavement.[31] Yet, as his long tirade against "the curse of service" (1.1.35) reveals, serving defines his identity as surely as it defines Othello's — if only by embittered negatives:

> We cannot all be masters, nor all masters
> Cannot be truly followed.

> Were I the Moor, I would not be Iago:
> In following him, I follow but myself.

> I am not what I am.
>   1.1.43–66

In this revolutionary deconstruction of official ideology, Iago boasts of serving Othello only "to serve my turn upon him," and of trimming himself "in forms and visages of duty . . . shows of service" only in order to "do [himself] homage" (ll. 42, 50–54). His "flag and sign of love" (1.1.157) is precisely the diabolical token of hypocrisy that the handbooks of domestic government taught their readers to expect in false servants, who (in Gouge's words) "have *a heart,* and a heart, making show of one heart outwardly, and have another, even a clean contrary heart within them" (617). Such servile hypocrites, according to Gouge and his fellow propagandist "I.M.," resemble "Judas, that false traitor, [who] . . . betray[ed] his own master, Christ," being "so possessed with a devil, as they will seek all the revenge they can, if they be corrected, [and] secretly endeavour to

---

[31] In a private communication David Evett has drawn my attention to the meticulousness with which Iago performs the role of ideal servant, carefully fulfilling even the most menial tasks assigned him.

Domestic service: an early seventeenth-century miniature watercolour,
depicting a servant bringing in dishes of food to a foursome of card-players.

take away the life of their masters."[32] Just as Doctor Faustus's surrender to the devil was couched in the language of egotistical self-
service ("The God thou *servest* is thine own appetite," A-Text,
2.1.11),[33] so Iago's rebellion is characterised as the self-homage of
one who acknowledges no "power and corrigible authority" save
that of his own "will" (1.3.326–27). The Ensign is someone who, for
all his obsession with "place" and "office," is at heart a "masterless
man" desiring to live (as the phrase had it) "at his own hand."[34] But
to be masterless, in an hierarchical order that defines each individual
as somebody's "man," was to be no man at all. Even Caliban's desire

[32] Gouge, 614, 617 and "I.M.," *A Health to the Gentlemanly Profession of Seruingmen*
(London, 1598), 148.

[33] Cited from Christopher Marlowe, *Doctor Faustus and Other Plays,* ed. David
Bevington and David Rasmussen (Oxford: Oxford University Press, 1995).

[34] See Paul Griffiths, "Masterless Young People in Norwich, 1560–1645," in Paul
Griffiths, Adam Fox, and Steve Hindle (eds.), *The Experience of Authority in
Early Modern England* (New York: St Martin's Press, 1996), 146–86 (154).

for "freedom" and to be "a new man" can be fulfilled only so long as he can claim "a new master" (*Tempest*, 2.1.185–87).

At once envying and detesting what he sees as his master's "free . . . nature" (1.3.393), Iago exploits it in order to enfetter the Moor to his own will. Yet, in one of many ironic reversals that characterise the structure of this tragedy, the word "slave," with which Montano, Othello, and Lodovico successively denounce him, symbolically degrades the Ensign to the very condition of "obsequious bondage" (1.1.46) from which his every action in the play was meant to free him. This is the condition he compares to the abject fate of "his master's ass" who "wears out his time . . . for naught but provender, and when he's old — cashier'd!" (1.1.47–48). Iago's figure slyly invokes the biblical type of virtuous disobedience, Balaam's ass, who defied his abusive master by appealing to a lifetime of dutiful service: "Am not I thine ass, upon which thou hast ridden ever since I was thine unto this day? was I ever wont to do so unto thee?" (Numbers, 22.30). But where the revolt of Balaam's patient beast was inspired by the angel of the lord, Iago's parodic unspeaking of the name of God ("I am not what I am"),[35] reminds us that *Non serviam* ("I will not serve") was the watchword of the fallen angel Lucifer and his rebellious cohorts. "In heav'n they scorned to *serve,* so now in hell they reign," wrote Phineas Fletcher of the rebel angels (*Purple Island* [1633], vi.10; emphasis added), anticipating the famous defiance of Milton's Satan: "Better to reign in hell, than *serve* in heaven" (*Paradise Lost;* i.263; emphasis added).[36] But where Lucifer asserts his independent selfhood by outright opposition to God, Iago's enigmatic taunt ironically betrays the self-undoing nature of his covert defiance.

---

[35] Ironically enough the Moor — having killed the wife whose love shaped his Venetian identity, his "occupation gone" and "chaos . . . come again" — at his lowest emotional point in the play, when he feels himself already in hell (5.2.275–78), will offer his own abject paraphrase of Iago's diabolic self-negation: "That's he that *was* Othello: here *I am.*" (l. 281) — where the reference of the final *I am* is confounded in advance by *he that was.*

24

Courtly service: an engraving of the Duc d'Alençon (one of Queen Elizabeth's royal suitors) shown on his ceremonial entrance into Antwerp.

The opposition between the idealised vision of service espoused by the Moor, and Iago's satanic *non serviam* establishes a complex framework for Emilia's disobedience — the action in which Strier discovers the "threshold" to *Lear.* This is especially so because her defiance extends beyond her husband, to include his (and her) "lord," Othello. Othello himself (like his "obedient" wife) remains a paradigm of honourable obedience: when he is "commanded home," even though it means the surrender of his "place" to his disgraced subordinate Cassio, he is quick to "obey the mandate" (4.1.260–63);

[36] Compare the faithful Abdiel's wish only to "*serve* / In heaven God ever blest, and his divine / Behests *obey*" (*Paradise Lost,* vi. 183–85; emphasis added). Satan's words constitute a diabolical travesty of the traditional formulae which insisted that to serve God was actually to rule (*cui servire regnare est,* in the words of the *Missa pro pacis* from the Sarum rite), and that (as the Benedictine Rule put it) it is "better to serve than to rule" — both cited in Evett, *op. cit.*

but when Emilia receives the same command from her domestic superior, she twice declines: "Perchance, Iago, I will ne'er go home. . . . I will not" (5.2.196, 221) — repeating, in effect, her husband's wilful repudiation of "corrigible authority." An act of deliberate self-estrangement from the domestic realm by which she is at once defined and confined, Emilia's refusal to return home constitutes a radical challenge to the very notions of propriety and property on which subordinate identity depends. Of course her disobedience is warranted, like Desdemona's repudiation of filial subservience by a "divided duty" (1.3.179) — "'Tis proper I obey him, but not now" (l. 195); but where Desdemona's allegiance was transferred to a new "lord," Emilia's love for her mistress compels her to defy both of the males who claim authority over her — her husband and her master too.

In the brothel scene, after Othello has redefined his "obedient lady" (4.1.248) as "that cunning whore of Venice" (4.2.88), Desdemona comes close to withdrawing allegiance when she feigns incomprehension of Emilia's reference to their "lord," declaring "I have none" (4.2.101). But the deferential language with which she greets her murderer in 5.2, together with her dying "Commend me to *my kind lord*" (ll. 24–25, 126), patiently reaffirms her subservience — to the point where the repeated "Lord" of her terrified pleading (ll. 57, 85) can seem to be addressed to her husband as much as to God. When Emilia first arrives at the scene of murder, she defers to Othello in the same language as her mistress, calling him "my lord," and "my good lord" (ll. 86, 91, 104, 107, 109, 113);[37] but, once he confesses to the murder, she sees him (in words that uncomfortably echo Iago's slanders at the beginning of the play) only as "black . . . devil," "most filthy bargain," "gull," "dolt as ignorant as dirt," "villain," "dull Moor," "murderous coxcomb," "fool," and "cruel Moor"

---

[37] The point is given particular emphasis in the Q text, where Desdemona's cry of "O Lord, Lord, Lord" mingles with Emilia's offstage "My lord, my lord . . . My lord, my lord" so that Othello seems almost unable to tell them apart: "What voice is this?" (5.2.85–87).

(ll. 132–247). Reducing her master once again to the contemptuous anonymity of "the Moor" she strips him of the respectful pronouns due from a subordinate, degrading him with the same contemptuous "thous" (ll. 134–36, 158–64, 197–98, 223, 247) that she uses to unspeak her husband's authority (ll. 171–73).

Emilia's rebellion belongs, then, to a painfully ironic circle, through which the initial contrast between idealised service and diabolical disobedience is acted out in reverse — the vicious *non serviam* of the masterless rebel being replayed as his wife's virtuous repudiation of patriarchal authority: "I will ne'er go home." By a similar inversion, through the cruel metamorphosis that converts the "rites" of matrimony into murder on the bed, Desdemona's desperately preserved allegiance to her "kind lord" produces only an absolute undoing of her identity, in which "nobody" becomes another name for "I myself." In much the same way, Othello's frantic attempt to re-make himself through a re-enactment of past service issues in an act of radical self-cancellation: for what else is his suicidal performance of revenge upon the malignant Turk who "Beat a Venetian and traduced the state" (5.2.350) but a brutal literalisation of Iago's "I am not what I am"?[38] It is to the extreme contradictions of Othello's last rhetorical performance and its "bloody period" that Gratiano's baffled paradox responds: "All that's spoke is marred" (l. 353). It is as if speech — traditionally both the signature of individual identity and the foundation of civil life in the *polis* — had learned to unspeak itself. No wonder that Lodovico orders the erasure of the unsettling spectacle on the bed, and, having confirmed Cassio's substitution in Othello's "place," ceremoniously reasserts his own role as official servant of Venice:

---

[38] I have been anticipated here by Eldred Jones, who notes that the "deliberate antithesis between what Iago is supposed to be and what he is ("I am not what I am") also occurs in Shakespeare's portrayal of Othello" — see Jones, *Othello's Countrymen: Africans in English Renaissance Drama* (Oxford: Oxford University Press, 1965), 109.

> Myself will straight aboard, and *to the state*
> This heavy act, with heavy heart relate.
>
> 5.2.366–67

If suicide, as Rosalie Colie once wrote, is "the paradox of self-contradiction at its irrevocable extremity,"[39] then Othello's drive to what he calls "my journey's end . . . [the] butt/ And very sea-mark of my utmost sail" (5.2.265–66) may be said to extend the contradictions of service to their self-cancelling limit. At the end of *King Lear*, the self-annihilating "journey" announced by the dutiful Earl of Kent, as he prepares to follow the dead king, is fraught with similar contradiction. The well-meaning, but ineffectual Albany has attempted to restore order with an appeal to public duty that recalls Lodovico's pious invocation of "the state" at the end of *Othello*. In what may seem like a disconcerting recapitulation of Lear's initial division of the kingdom, the Duke summons Edgar and Kent to joint authority in the realm:

> Friends of my soul, you twain
> Rule in this realm, and the gor'd *state* sustain.
>
> *King Lear,* 5.3.329–30

But, in contrast to Lodovico's choric couplet, Albany's conspicuously fails to achieve even the rhetorical closure that its form encodes. Edgar, though sounding again "the note of obedience" observed by Barish and Waingrow, does so only by a kind of equivocation that sidesteps the very issues of authority and service with which the tragedy has been so obsessively concerned — "The weight of this *sad time* we must *obey*" (l. 323).[40] The blunt-speaking Kent,

[39] Rosalie Colie, *Paradoxia Epidemica: The Renaissance Tradition of Paradox* (Princeton, NJ: Princeton University Press, 1966), 486.

[40] F, as Muir suggests, is surely right in giving this speech to Edgar, rather than to Albany (as in Q). Richard Strier (123) emphasises the way in which Edgar's lines, setting "what we *feel*" against "what we *ought* to say" (l. 324), echo "the paradoxical conception of obedience through breaching normal decorum" that is so recurrent a feature of the play.

by contrast, responds to Albany with an absolute refusal, insisting that his duty lies unanswerably elsewhere.

> I have a journey, sir, shortly to go;
> My master calls me, I must not say no.
>
> ll. 321–22

Kent, the humble journey-man, says no by insisting that no is what he must not say. What are we to make of this resolute, but paradoxical demurral — coming as it does from a man whose fortunes in the play have been wholly determined by his defiant negation of his master's will in the opening scene? The answer is to be found partly in the play's larger treatment of service and obedience, and partly in the contradictions that characterise Kent's own performance of his servant role.

King Lear, as Barish and Waingrow showed, is built around a set of oppositions (even more elaborate than those of *Othello*) between the exponents of false and true service — between the mercenary time-servers mocked by the fool, who "serve and seek for gain, / And follow but for form"(2.4.72–73, 78–79), and those faithful servants whose willingness, if need be, to "break [their] neck with following" is played out through their physical following of the King in his demented progress through the wasteland of houseless (and therefore masterless) wretches that takes the place of his kingdom. In this scheme it is Edmund, the man with "service" constantly on his lips,[41] who emerges as Iago's most obvious counterpart. Edmund begins the play with a courtly tender of "services" to Kent and a promise to "study deserving" (1.1.29–31). But just as Iago's opening tirade declares his intention to follow Othello only "to serve my turn upon him," so Edmund's first soliloquy announces that his "services are bound" only to "Nature" (1.2.1–2), the "Goddess" who stands (like Faustus's God) only for his own appetite, the egotistic desires licensed by his identity as a "natural son."[42]

---

[41] Barish and Waingrow, 350.

[42] See Michael Neill, "'In Everything Illegitimate': Imagining the Bastard in English Renaissance Drama," in *Putting History to the Question*, 127–148 (138).

Thus the "loyal service" for which Edmund is praised (4.2.7) amounts in the end to no more than the sexual "services" he exchanges with his "mistress," Goneril, and her sister Regan, whose unnatural "lord and master" he becomes (4.2.21–27, 5.3.78–79). Goneril's go-between in this business is another exemplar of false service, her flattering steward Oswald — prophetically identified by Kent as "one that [would] be a bawd in way of good service" (2.2.18–19), and denounced by Edgar as "a serviceable villain, / As duteous to the vices of [his] mistress / As badness would desire" (4.6.254–56). To Goneril, Oswald is her "trusty servant" (4.2.19), but to Kent a mere "slave," one of those abject time-servers who "Renege, affirm, and turn their halcyon beaks / With every gale and vary of their masters, / Knowing nought, like dogs, but following" (ll. 73, 79–81). Kent's contemptuous epithets echo the indignant language of the sixteenth-century music-teacher, Thomas Whythorne, who, refusing to be a pliant "water-spaniel" to his employer, thought it "a slave-like and servile trade to be a flatterer, for . . . like as the shadow followeth a man continually wheresoever he doth go, so a flatterer applieth to crouch, follow, and please, when he thinketh to gain any good thereby."[43] Such abject, dog-like obedience, Kent suggests, is a form of false service that can only destroy the sacred bonds by which the household (and thus the whole social order) is held together: "Such smiling rogues as these, / Like rats, oft bite the holy cords a-twain / Which are too intrince t'unloose" (2.2.74–76). Yet Kent himself is a man whose deliberate disobedience at the beginning of the play has, from an orthodox perspective at least, already loosened the "holy cords" that bind servant to master.

Kent is foremost amongst those, like Gloucester and Cornwall's servant, who discover the moral limits of compliance, and (in contrast to the retinue of "silly-ducking observants" sneered at by Cornwall) insist upon upholding those limits even at the risk of their own lives. It is Cornwall's nameless manservant who, though

---

[43] James M. Osborn (ed.), *The Autobiography of Thomas Whythorne* (London: OUP, 1962), 53.

dismissed by his master as a "slave" or mere chattel — "*My* villain!" (3.7.77) — is made to assert the freedom of his conscience by articulating the paradox of "virtuous disobedience" that is central to Strier's account of the play:

> I have serv'd you ever since I was a child,
> But better service have I never done you
> Than now to bid you hold.
>
> 3.7.72–74

As important as the paradox itself, is the Servant's appeal to the intimacy of early modern service: together with the Messenger's later description of the servant as one that Cornwall himself "bred," this speech acts as a reminder of the naturalised ties that made the words *household* and *family* virtually interchangeable. "Bred," after all, is the same word that Cordelia uses in defining the "bond" between father and child at the moment of her own defiance:

> Good my Lord,
> You have begot me, *bred* me, lov'd me: I
> Return those duties back as are right fit,
> Obey you, love you and most honour you.
>
> 1.1.95–98

In this way the servant's rebellion implicitly invites comparison with the tempestuous confrontation of the opening scene, where the King's rebellious subordinate unites with his recalcitrant child in opposition to the royal will. In that episode, too, the close resemblance of filial and servantly bonds was emphasised by the language of Kent's intervention against the King's disinheritance of Cordelia:

> Royal Lear,
> Whom I have ever honour'd as my King,
> Lov'd as my father, as my master follow'd,
> As my great patron thought on in my prayers —
>
> 1.1.139–42

The incantatory syntax of this speech, linking the roles of king, master, patron, and father, is dense with the assumptions of patriarchal thought, which stressed the paternal role of monarchs, even as it insisted on the sovereign authority of heads of household within their domestic realms. The sacralized nature of service, implicit in Kent's deferential honorifics, is underlined by his use of "patron" — literally a surrogate father, but a term with religious connotations that are animated by "thought on in my prayers." Kent, however — by insisting, like Cordelia, that love and duty cannot be coterminous with obedience — invokes the sacredness of service only (it seems) to violate it. Cordelia's conviction that her bond itself defines the exact bounds — "no more nor less" — of obligation (ll. 92–93), is amplified in the Earl's allegory of honourable resistance, where the heavy metrical stress on "falls" identifies Lear's metamorphosis from King to Fool as a virtual deposition:

> Think'st thou that Duty shall have dread to speak
> When Power to Flattery bows. To Plainness
> 　　　　　　　　　　Honour's bound,
> When Majesty *falls* to Folly.
> 　　　　ll. 147–49[44]

It diminishes both the power of this scene and the impact of the whole tragedy to assume, as Strier does, that Kent's revolt must command the immediate and unequivocal endorsement of the audience. The courtier's public defiance, like the daughter's stubborn negatives, is meant to shock. Indeed Kent's own language (together with Lear's response) makes it clear that such resistance, however virtuously motivated, involves a *de facto* repudiation of "allegiance" (l. 167). The man he first addressed with proper deference as "my Liege," "Royal Lear," and "my King" (ll. 120, 139–40), is now hailed (as Emilia hailed Othello) with the insulting intimacy of the singular pronoun (ll. 146–81), and (in a rhetorical anticipation of the political and literal divestiture to come) reduced to bare

---

[44] I have altered the capitalisation in Kent's speech in order to point up the allegorical schema, according to which Kent identifies himself with Duty or Honour, Cordelia with Plainness (or Truth), her sisters with Flattery, and Lear with Power or Majesty turned to Folly.

King Lear on the Heath *(1767) by Alexander Runciman. Lear is attended by Kent in disguise, the Fool and Edgar as Poor Tom.*

"Lear," and "old man." No wonder, then, that in the King's eyes Kent becomes (in terms suggestive not merely of feudal betrayal, but of religious heresy and apostasy) a "miscreant" or "recreant" (ll. 161, 166) — one whose repudiation of obedience appears almost as monstrous as Cordelia's seeming violation of the filial bond. Just as "paternal care, / Propinquity, and property of blood" are formally withdrawn from the unfilial daughter (ll. 113–14), so the protection of the royal law is withdrawn from the revolted vassal (ll. 176–79). Each is rendered, in the deepest sense, "a stranger to my heart and me" (l. 115) — a curse that Lear renders "sacred" by calling on the Gods, Hecate and Apollo (ll. 110, 159) to endorse his sentence.

The original power of this scene must have depended on its ability to animate the strains and contradictions apparent in early modern attitudes towards service and obedience. On the one hand Kent's resistance to the "excesse" of the King's authority, could capitalise on the radical theories espoused by Buchanan and others and appeal to the discontents of men like Thomas Whythorne, for whom the obligations of service had begun to feel like tyranny; on the other — as the apocalyptic imagery of Gloucester's ensuing meditation on the cracking of natural "bonds" suggests (1.2.107–23) — the audience were meant to feel the profoundly destructive potential of Kent's violation of deferential taboo. For the vassal's repudiation of service amounts to a desacralization of royal authority — something that, as Shakespeare had already shown in *Richard II,* could not easily be reversed. Indeed, scarcely has the rebellious Kent been banished from the King's retinue, than the bonds of service begin to unravel with Goneril's instructions to Oswald and his fellows to exercise "a weary negligence" towards her father — "If you come slack of former services, / You shall do well" (1.3.10–14). Whatever the motives for Kent's defiance, it visibly initiates the process by which Lear is symbolically denuded of the "train" of followers essential to the preservation of his royal "countenance" and the "authority" it expresses (1.4.29–30, 255–60, 303–4; 2.4.239–65)[45] — to the point where, in the storm scene, the King feels himself in thrall to those "servile ministers" of his daughters' malign will, the elements, against which he will oppose his desecrated nakedness: "You owe me no subscription: then let fall / Your horrible pleasure; here I stand, your slave" (3.2.18–21).

Thus, however virtuous Kent's disobedience may seem to us, it nonetheless involves a kind of sacrilege for which the play will

---

[45] The double sense of "train" makes a king's retinue effectively an extension of royal costume, like the trailing ends of "robes and furred gowns," so that the loss of his servants is quite literally part of the process of reducing Lear to the nakedness of Act 4.

require him to do penance; and if Lear's progress through the play is often understood as a kind of purgatory, then Kent's journey (including his humiliation in the stocks) resembles a penitential pilgrimage, in which the fallen servant is redeemed only by submitting himself to what Edgar will call "service / Improper for a slave" (5.3.220–21), his degradation humiliatingly marked by the acceptance of money from the King as "an earnest of [his] service" (1.2.99). However, whereas Kent's *non serviam* begins to dissolve the familiar hierarchy of obedience, his return as the humble manservant, "Caius," determined to "serve where [he does] stand condemn'd" (1.4.5), introduces what will emerge as an antic double of the royal household: he is joined in succession by the Fool — whose schooling of Kent as he sits in the stocks identifies him as a second avatar of self-sacrificial service (2.4.67–85); by Edgar, who claims to be another disgraced "servingman, proud in heart and mind" — one who (like Oswald or Edmund) "serv'd the lust of my mistress' heart" (3.4.65–66); and finally by Gloucester whose sense of duty to the King compels his fatal disobedience to the "hard commands" of Goneril and Reagan (3.4.152–53).

Kent, whose disguise enables him to transform his life into a virtual allegory of obedient service, is the key figure in this schema: in "[s]erv[ing] the King" he makes himself once again, as every good servant should, simply part of his presence, so that any assault on himself becomes an attack "Against the grace and person of my master" (2.2.129–32). Challenged by Lear to identify himself, Kent answers simply "a man" — a claim that implicitly links his very humanity to his dependent role as the King's "man": and when Lear asks him what he seeks, Kent answers with the single word, "service," that defines both "what" he is ("who" being no longer of any concern to him) and the limit of all that he could possibly desire. He will "profess" service (ll. 12–15) as another might profess faith. The King, he declares, using a term that will become increasingly resonant as the action unfolds, has "that in [his] countenance that I would fain call *master*" — namely "authority" (ll. 30–32). That alone can authorise him as the proper "creature" (or creation) of royal favour, confirming his proper servantly identity as a part of Lear's regal "countenance."

"Master" is, of course, the same richly resonant word with which Kent, at last abandoning his base disguise, and coming (as he says) "To bid my King and *master* aye goodnight" (5.2.235), will announce his formal return to the court from which he was expelled in the opening scene; and it is also the word with which he will justify his departure from the play-world. Edgar, similarly stripped of his antic guise and arrayed once more in his true nobility as Gloucester's heir, has praised the constancy with which Kent "Follow'd his enemy king, and did him service / Improper for a slave" (5.3.220–21). However, Kent's decision to shed his servile livery and show himself, as Cordelia urged, "better suited" (4.7.6), hardly confirms Edgar's straightforward understanding of social propriety. Indeed the Earl is at pains to stress the seamless continuity between his base and noble roles: greeting the King not with the flattering honorifics which the fool has mocked as "court holy-water" (3.2.10), but with a repetition of the commonplace term that defines his own humble dependency — "my good master!" (5.3.267) — he insists that "Your servant Kent" and "your servant Caius" are indistinguishable, since "I am the *very man* . . . That from your first of difference and decay, / Have follow'd your sad steps" (ll. 283–89). Kent thus proclaims himself unchangeably "the same" (l. 282); yet his claim rests on an unsustainable paradox: the very "difference" that he has committed himself to follow (a difference partly of his own making), means that neither he, nor the idea of service for which he stands, can ever be "the same" again. His transformation, whatever Albany may wish, can no more be reversed than Lear can be restored by the "fresh garments" in which his daughter has reinvested him.

In his deep conviction of the sacred nature of service, the Earl turns to the unanswerable language of vocation to announce his determination to attend his dead lord on his final progress: "My *master* calls me, I must not say no" (5.2.321–22). Among the scriptural texts remembered in this deceptively bare speech are the scribe's words to Jesus in Matthew 8.19 ("Master, I wil followe thee whethersoeuer thou goest"), Martha's to Mary in John 11.28 ("the Master is come, and calleth for thee"), and (above all) Jesus's own words in St John's gospel, where he defines true service by the willingness to follow him out of this world: "He that loueth his life, shal lose it; and he that hateth his life in this worlde, shal keepe it vnto life eternal. If anie man *serue* me, let him followe me; for where I am, there shal also my *seruant* be: and if anie man *serue* me, him wil my Father honour" (12.25–26; emphasis added). This last echo is made even more powerful by the fact that the scriptural passage immediately follows St John's account of the resurrection of Lazarus — the episode that is so bleakly deconstructed in Lear's agony over Cordelia's corpse:

> she lives! if it be so,
> It is a chance which does redeem all sorrows
> That ever I have felt.
> 5.3.265–67

But the very desolation of this spectacle of failed redemption is a reminder that Kent's appeal to the ethos of sacralized service is made in a desacralized world where no correspondence can be demonstrated between human order and the arbitrary powers that Lear once saw manifested in "the sacred radiance of the sun" (1.1.109). The pious resolution of Kent's "journey" will lead him out of the play-world into a space that seems defined only by the litany of appalled negation that, with unalterable finality, reinstates the sullen "nothing" of the opening scene:

> . . . . Thou'lt come no more,
> Never, never, never, never, never!
> ll. 307–8

ABOUT THE AUTHOR

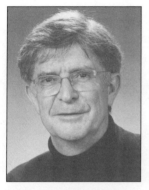 Michael Neill was born in Tenby, South Wales in 1942. He spent the early part of his life in Ireland until 1955, when his family returned to New Zealand. He was educated at the University of Otago before proceeding to postgraduate work at the University of Cambridge. Now Professor of English at the University of Auckland (where he has taught since 1967), he is the author of *Issues of Death: Mortality and Identity in English Renaissance Tragedy* (Oxford University Press, 1997), and *Putting History to the Question: Power, Politics, and Society in English Renaissance Drama* (Columbia University Press, 2000), a selection from his numerous essays on early modern literature. He has edited *Anthony and Cleopatra* for the Oxford Shakespeare, and is currently completing an edition of *Othello* for the same series. His other research interests include Restoration Literature, Postcolonial Fiction, and Irish Literature.